STRIZHOV

The Enigmatic World of Dmitri Strizhov

Robert C. Morgan

Global Curiosity

Special Thanks to Elena Tchernichova, Lou Christie,
John Narins, Ann Kjellberg, Charles and Christine Prince

Copyright © 1998 by Dmitri Strizhov, Global Curiosity, Inc.
The Enigmatic World of Dmitri Strizhov/by Robert C. Morgan
Editor Rita Bernhard
Concept by Dmitri Strizhov
Photo by Peter Gritsyk
Design by Dmitri Strizhov, Mirek Nisenbaum, Ed Kabatsky, Aleksandr Tochilovsky

Published by Global Curiosity, Inc.

First Edition 1998
ISBN 0-9662641-0-x
Global Curiosity, Inc.
3535 US Route 1
Princeton, NJ 08540 U.S.A.

Printed in Singapore

Dedicated to Elena Tchernichova

The Enigmatic World of Dmitry Strizhov

by Robert C. Morgan

Dmitry Strizhov is a young Russian-born painter who lives in a world entirely of his own making. It is a mythological world filled with colorful figures in imaginary landscapes, a world that has been turned upside down as shown in the enigmatic faces he loves to paint. Yet there is a certain heroism in his mythical world, a heroism that opens the door to the unconscious in a playful way.

One may talk about a considerable breadth of emotions discussed in the pictorial juxtapositions of these paintings. Their craftlike precision lends authenticity to the projection of feelings that range from pathos to a Dionysian abandon. Strizhov's exuberant paintings combine figurative and abstract elements through the use of modeling techniques that are juxtaposed with brilliant planes of primary and secondary colors. He is a poet in both visual and literary terms.

One is impelled to examine Strizhov's situation from two interrelated points of view: the aesthetic and the political. First, his aesthetics are not calculated so much as given a necessary form of empathy. Put another way, he is not struggling for some aspect of classical form of aesthetics contingent on perfection in the universe of beauty. Rather, he is interested in playfulness, a quality more given to his romantic temperament. Through the process of play he sets up a certain dialectical tension, a force of visual opposites in perpetual tension with each other. This quality of play emerges repeatedly in Strizhov's images as one examines the intricacies in these delightful paintings. One is reminded of the late German critic, Walter Benjamin, who wrote in great seriousness about play, particularly as manifested in children's toys. In his *Moscow Diary*, Benjamin discusses in aesthetic detail how the colors and shapes of these Russian toys capture not only images of the unconscious but also the power of the creative imagination.

Dmitry Strizhov's political story is symptomatic of much that has happened over the past decade in the changing course of world politics. Born in St. Petersburg (then called Leningrad) in 1967, Strizhov witnessed the collapse of the former Communist state when he was in his early twenties. St. Petersburg, its traditional name now restored, remains an important center of Russian cultural history, but Strizhov believed that remaining in that city would not advance his artistic career.

Thus he emigrated to the United States where he lives today.

Although he had established a certain reputation as both a painter and poet, he felt that the provincial aspect of life in Russia was too deeply entrenched in its own history and inflexible standards of taste, not unlike nineteenth-century Vienna. In contrast to St. Petersburg (which Strizhov has painted in his own fanciful way), Vienna was able to generate an aesthetic break from its typically exorbitant decorative, provincial style through the secession movement at the end of the century. The secession happened largely through artists and architects intent on reaching out to other European influences, including the United Kingdom. On the other hand, St. Petersburg, with its flourishing tradition in the plastic arts over the centuries, was less able to relinquish its foothold on history and the embedded aspect of its traditional aesthetics.

Strizhov made the decision to move to the United States in the early nineties, a time when it was relatively easy to make such a transition in one's artistic career. He was young enough to avoid the sentimentality and concomitant resentment of looking back at his Russian past. Instead, he began reconstructing an identity for himself in New York. While energetic work played an important role in Strizhov's career, one cannot ignore his emotional will, his shrewd intelligence, and his ability to seize opportunities. In 1990 the time was right.

The artist took advantage of this moment in Russian history to move into a new situation. Despite America's emphasis on commercial values (an emphasis not entirely antithetical to many Russians), it was here that he found a democratic platform on which to stand and a place to work where art did not stand still.

Several Ways to Keep Up One's End of the Conversation

Although English is Dmitry Strizhov's second language, it is not the essence of his thought. His thought is his vision, the origin of his imaginative paintings. The colors and shapes he pours into his pictures make his droll figures come alive. Perhaps they are the result of the artist thinking in Russian. One might surmise that Strizhov "imagines" in Russian as well. There is an inescapable attachment to one's first language. The penetration of thought and formulation of a visual idea emerge through that first language. As a poet, Strizhov is forever in search of the right word, the right color, in order to establish the proper nuance.

In one of Strizhov's recent paintings, entitled *Several Ways to Keep Up One's End of the Conversation*, two figures are positioned side by side.

One is seated, the other is not. Yet the two are inextricably bound in their language, their manner of speaking, their gestures, their facial nuances. There is a feeling of repose, a kind of subtlety about the manner in which they are intertwined, suggesting intimacy, as though the conversation had suddenly turned to the interior meaning of things. This is not a casual conversation, but a vibrant exchange of words and feelings. The bright colors are surrogates for the texture of the dialogue.

The upper left region of the canvas is itself a discrete painting, an abstraction. The upper right—a mottled light green—descends over the shoulders of the seated figure. Untextured colors enter into the wardrobes of the two figures: purple, light cerulean, orange, green, and brown. There is virtually no empty space. The surface is typical of Strizhov's stylistic motif in that he persistently uses color like a jigsaw puzzle. It is a method of painting that removes any trace of classical intent.

Another typical motif in Strizhov's paintings are the fingers he creates; they resemble vegetables, biomorphic shapes reminiscent of turnips, roots from the earth. They are organic. There are virtually no hands. The fingers push through the sleeves of the tunic. They reach or point, but not in the classical sense of expression. These biomorphic tendrils, these rootlike fingers, betray a kind of eroticism that finds its equivalent in the soil of the earth. This mannerism suggests that Strizhov is bound to a primitive or naive style of painting, a literary genre that has been given a pictorial form. It is difficult to classify his paintings in purely modernist terms. His paintings revert to a form of primitivism not unrelated to the early works of the Russian suprematist Kazimir Malevich, who painted between 1909 and 1910. One might speculate that Strizhov's affinity to primitivism is a means toward finding an unconscious referent for his work in early twentieth-century Russian art. Although this cannot be ascertained, his method of obsessional painting with clear contours and shapes indeed links the artist to a tradition and allows him to project his visual concerns in a direction that offers a new lyricism. In general, Strizhov's primitivism is about reestablishing a sense of personal myth in painting.

Assuming that this painting is about conversation, we also understand that the artist is searching for a reference, a meaning that exists outside his formal vocabulary. In a sense, Strizhov uses a formal vocabulary—one that is thoroughly understood—to get into another world, another reality, another personal mythology that allows his own vocabulary of images to spring forth. This is the job of the real artist. This is what separates the inventive artist from the academician. It is the ability to invent a new vocabulary of imagery, but it is also about giving these images an inventive syntax, that is, finding the right conjugation through highly intuitive means. Strizhov is perpetually in search of this conjugation. His desire is one of intuitively coming to terms with the most accurate syntax within his pictorial means.

In *Several Ways to Keep Up One's End of the Conversation*, there is the search for a formal means that is unmistakable in its allure. It is a painting about language, about the exchange of words between two individuals. There is a certain irony, however, in all this. The title of the painting suggests a struggle. Strizhov is a Russian-born artist struggling to understand the terms of another society. Not only is it a struggle to come to terms with American society, but he must come to terms as well with the New York cultural establishment. Thus he is trying "to keep up"—to maintain his end of the conversation. He is the listener, but he is also the artist who is expected to have something to say. He has to distinguish between what is significant and what is not. There is a gap between cocktail chatter, for example, and a more searching intimate discussion. With the terms of the latter, the artist has to understand the subtleties of feeling, the innuendoes, all the gestures and intonations.

This is a painting that encapsulates a simple metaphor of common language—the Russian artist struggling to keep up his end of the conversation with a certain diligence, a noble effort, knowing that his mythical world of feeling is contingent on how effectively he is able to express what he means at any given time, at any given place. In many ways this is a personal painting of the artist's dilemma in dealing with the intimacy of exchange, the struggle to ferret out a means to express what is beyond language, to understand what he is hearing and what he has just understood. It is a painting about the language of intimacy in a new cultural context, and, in many ways, it is a key to Strizhov's dilemma: the raw material that gives all his work the specific poignancy that reaches out to the individual viewer.

The Neo-Primitive Impulse

Dmitry Strizhov studied painting at the Leningrad Academy of Fine Arts from 1979 to 1984 with Professor Evgeny Antonov, one of the former Soviet Union's notable artists and teachers. During his years at the academy, Strizhov learned a gamut of techniques and formal processes that enabled him to free himself, once he left school, of the obvious practices of the academic style. His first important group exhibition outside the Soviet Union was held in 1988 in West Berlin, the year before the wall dividing that city would crumble. The following year he was included in two group exhibitions in Leningrad and another in New York. In 1990 he moved to New York, and his paintings appeared in exhibitions in San Francisco and in Danbury, Connecticut. The following year (1991) he established an association with the

Ergane Gallery in New York and was included in a small group exhibition at the prestigious Albright-Knox Art Gallery in Buffalo, New York. Strizhov's style of figuration has an illustrational aspect to it, almost childlike and not unrelated to the kind of rendering one might see in children's books. Some art historians may choose to refer to this type of painting as naive or "primitive." Although the term *primitive* has become controversial in recent years, it is still a useful epithet if understood within its proper context. Primitive painting—at least in the sense that Malevich appropriated it in his early years—was a style of painting used by untrained folk artists to express emotional content directly. Instead of following the painstaking rigors of academic formalism, primitivism was intent on bypassing the rules in order to get to the core of one's emotional state of being. This method was, of course, appropriated by the early German expressionists as well—namely, Die Brucke (1905-1912) in Dresden—and eventually by the Swiss artist Paul Klee, an original member, along with the Russian artist Kandinsky of Der Blaue Reiter, which was established a few years later in Munich.

Klee was especially involved in a childlike approach to painting in his late career when he attempted to simulate as closely as possible the process of making child art a form of direct pictorial (linear) representation. The term *primitive*, therefore, has three meanings. It may refer to a method or style of image making used by either untrained artists, schizophrenics, or children, as in the work of Klee. Another archaic usage implies that primitive art is the kind of pictorial representation made in "primitive" cultures. This is a less satisfactory application of the term and is ultimately false. Anyone who has attempted to investigate African sculpture, for example, the exquisite Benin bronzes, may conclude that these works are as sophisticated formally as any works known in the history of European, American, or Asian art.

Strizhov has a certain "primitive" aspect to his paintings, as noted earlier, in his persistent use of bright, flat primary and secondary colors, in his depiction of hands as roots, and in his use of the askance turning of the head using basic childlike expressions. To call Strizhov's paintings "neo-primitive" would not be misleading if one accepts the basic concept of a formal naivete. He is neither untrained, insane, nor consciously childlike. Like Klee, and to a certain extent the early Kandinsky, Strizhov deploys all the academic training he acquired to vary in subtle ways the method he used to construct a composition. His compositions are never formally obvious. Consider, for example *Orange Cat* and *Revelry on the Level of Historic Days*. One may investigate both these paintings from the position of a formal naivete. The orange cat in the former painting is humorously attached to the side of a barren tree, and the humanoid figure with head twisted in reverse appears to be in a state of reverie. The railing behind the bend in *Orange Cat* is acutely sophisticated in its modeling, its mixing of color, and its gradation. This might be seen in contrast to the intense blue, red, and green shapes that describe the sitter's costume. Or, for that matter, consider the pink embankment that flows like a wave across the background of the horizon and meets the turquoise sky— also painted in a flat color. The relationship of the modeling on the railing with these flat colors, juxtaposed as they are, suggest that Strizhov is clearly aware of how he is utilizing his academic training as a painter to create something new and vibrant that falls outside normal categories in figurative painting.

Much the same can be said of *Revelry on the Level of Historic Days*. Here the figure is seated against a wall with the title in English inscribed on it. He is holding what appears to be a child wrapped up in his tunic. To the lower right is a tree stump that is transformed into the top of an Ionian column. Again there is the mixture of the intense flat color with the modeling, the primitive appearance with the academic subtlety. The point is that although Strizhov appears to be a primitive, one cannot discount his awareness of these formal devices that he repeats over and over again as a means to push certain aspects of his mythological content. In a purely technical sense, one might find a curious relationship with another Russian painter from the preceding generation, also living in New York, named Michael Odnoralov. Although the two differ vastly in their content and approach to rendering the figure, Odnoralov uses a similar method of flat planes of color in relation to the modeling figure. It would be impossible to call Odnoralov a "primitive." On the other hand, Strizhov does paint with a childlike impulse that persists through a unique style of visual lyricism. The term *neo-primitive* implies that he has discovered a kind of synthesis between naive content and formal training, yet one that is more than the sum of its parts. His undetermined pictorial compositions give the work a unique resonance and projection of feeling. It is this special quality, combined with the deployment of a formal means, that makes Strizhov's paintings so ineluctably engaging.

Stage Set for Vienna State Ballet Production of "Don Quixote"
Choreography by Elena Tchernichova

Classical Ballet

The medium of dance and choreography has been a natural evolution
in Strizhov's work over the past five years. Beginning in 1992 he was
commissioned to execute a curtain design and stage sets for the oper-
atic version of Miguel Cervantes's *Don Quixote* at the Vienna State
Opera Ballet. Given that earlier commissions had been handed to such
artists as Miro, Picasso, and Chagall, this was a considerable boon to
Strizhov's career. His illustrational propensity as one aspect of his
enormous artistic output became exceedingly clear, especially in the
curtain design. Many of the formal techniques present in his oil paintings were given a new large-scale format. The dynamic richness of the
color—Strizhov's trademark—radiated with vibrancy and virtuosity
across the proscenium of the stage. The viewer witnesses in abstract

form the romantic figure of Quixote surrounded by his lover, his henchman, and his horse—all major characters in this classical drama—as a multicolored ensemble.

Strizhov's sense of dramaturgy and his acute ability to choreograph figures within a pictorial space make his venture into stage design quite natural. Two other paintings, *Ballet* and *Classical Ballet*, reinforce this ability. The former is the most conventional and illustrative, whereas the latter verges on the surreal. In *Ballet* a single male figure, dressed in an ochre tunic and green and blue vest, is positioned against a pink wall. A child's ball appears in the lower right. On the left side of the wall, an abstract village can be seen in the distance—a motif Chagall also used in many of his early paintings, thus signaling a reverie or reminiscence of the Russian village. On the other hand, *Classical Ballet* has a more perverse aspect. Instead of one figure, there are two. Their demeanor is less strident than in the painting *Ballet*. They stand in the foreground, looming heavily across the picture plane. Their turnip-fingered hands are enormous and somewhat threatening. The figures are not so much engaged in movement as they are preparing to move, an eerie pas de deux perhaps. The arms, shoulders, and fingers are a single organ, a mutation, fastidiously rendered—clearly related to works by Dali or Max Ernst. The figure on the left displays a craggy, torn shape as if a collage element had been affixed to his torso. This suggests a psychic disturbance, emotional distress, related to the expressionism of Baselitz.

The line between surrealism and primitivism—often the source of much controversy in twentieth-century art—is not always a clear one. For example, Strizhov's *Classical Ballet* sublimates the unconscious, on the one hand, and the deliberately perverse, on the other. In so doing, the artist creates an aura in his painting that verges on some biomorphic form of science fiction. Given the extraordinary flood of information and vicarious experiences to which human beings are routinely subjected in our current age, Strizhov's visual argument appears logical, if not somewhat reactionary. This dilemma is evident in many of the paintings discussed in this essay in that they exist somewhere between the surrealist and what I have labeled the neo-primitivist positions. Having suggested earlier that Strizhov is not clearly connected to the modernist avant-garde, it is no wander that surrealism, being an aberration of modernism, and primitivism, a decidedly "premodernist" position, have both entered into the artist's visual vocabulary. What is curious, however, is how the theme of dance—with all its classical stature and its relationship to Russian culture—became the ploy by which the artist chose to sublimate his desires, to give them a jolt through his superrational endeavor to construct formally a picture, an ironic symbol of the ballet that is so perfectly fitting for an ironic age of chaotic communication.

Color Relationship with Katherine B.

In 1993, three years after settling in New York, Dmitry Strizhov exhibited

a series of paintings entitled *The Color Relationship with Katherine B.*

in a one-man exhibition at the Ergane Gallery (a.k.a. Develin Gallery)

in Soho. This is one of the most enigmatic groups of paintings of

the artist's young career. In the exhibition brochure Alisa Tager describes

the general features of the artist's work—the multicolored shapes, the

twisted heads, the disjointed bodies—paying particular attention to

the performative aspect of the work as seen in the painting *Woman*

with a Masque, one of the most compelling works from this exhibition.

Tager perceptively asserts that Strizhov's "off-beat images and sce-

narios are strange caricatures of an inexplicable reality." What is interesting, however, is how deeply one might psychologically analyze this series of works devoted to the allusive character of the show's main protagonist, the elusive and mysterious Katherine B.

Strizhov has essentially created a mythological figure—a feminine persona, in fact—who participates in various settings and situations. She is a repository of feelings and glances, expectations and observations. Katherine B. is a made-up name, a fictitious character, yet a distinct presence lingering in the artist's mind. The nineteenth-century French novelist Honore' de Balzac often spoke so vividly about his fictitious characters that his friends were uncertain as to whether these characters actually existed. A similar uncertainty—or mystery—surrounds Katherine B. She weaves through these paintings as if held by some invisible aura or, for that matter, as if she were a character in an ongoing soap opera. She exists as an overt representation of a woman, voyeuristically observed in her solitude, as in the title painting for the exhibition, *The Color Relationship with Katherine B.*

Conversely Katherine B. also exists through her absence, as in the humorous (even symbolic) *Dog Pondering Katherine B.* Another form of absence is in the context of a conversation—a theme Strizhov has represented in several of his paintings. In *Alina in Conversation with Katherine B.* there is a single figure behind a gnarled tree without leaves—another element in the artist's perpetually additive vocabulary of signs. Is it Alina who is symbolically represented? If so, where is Katherine B? Which one is depicted in the painting? One might assume that the viewer is confronting Alina behind the gnarled tree, but not necessarily. Is Katherine B. peering out at the viewer? There is a similar conundrum in relation to the reddish husky in *Dog Pondering Katherine B*. The assumption is that this obtrusive canine is peering at Katherine B.

Consider a fourth painting entitled *Trepidation with Which Katherine B. Has Parted*. This further enhances the mystery of this alluring feminine persona. The viewer perceives the single figure in the painting in the center of her village. She is blond, her head twisted to one side, her hands with turnip fingers, and again she is peering out at the viewer. Is this Katherine B. or are we arbitrarily experiencing the absence of Katherine B? Does this mysterious woman resemble Duchamp's "Rrose Selavy"—an alter ego? The answer is not clear.

Nor is it clear whether Strizhov is representing himself as a feminine absence. Assuming that to be the case, the artist is being playful with a psychological concept closely linked to post-Freudian psychology and particularly evident in the work of Jacques Lacan, namely, transference; that is, the viewer of the painting redirects his or her feelings and desires retained from childhood toward the objects in the painting. Katherine B. may be the artist's female persona. We do not know this, however, and it is not meant to be known. Yet there is the alluring

sensation that perhaps Strizhov himself carries this persona as a

means to engage the viewer in a special kind of dialogue, a transfer-

ence, where in fact the viewer suddenly and arbitrarily becomes the

subject of the painting.

Toward Abstraction

The argument is frequently made that at the end of this century the polar division between representational painting and abstract painting no longer exists. What existed at the outset of this century was, for the most part, a clear-cut separation. Mondrian, for example, argued in favor of "abstract reality" in contrast to what he called "natural reality." Eventually he wanted to surpass even the abstract and move into the realm of what he called "pure plastic painting," that is, painting that had the power to signify spiritual values, painting that would take the viewer outside the reality of mundane objects and incite a feeling of transcendence. Even Malevich argued in favor of his suprematist painting once he left primitivism and cubo-futurism behind. The new painting, for Malevich, was the purely nonobjective, that which existed on its own terms and carried the weight of spiritual values, what Malevich called "the desert"—being the signifier of emptiness that would incite spiritual contemplation on the part of the viewer. There are, of course, numerous other examples.

Today these divisions no longer are appropriate. One cannot so easily distinguish between what is representational and what is abstract. The case for their conjugation is succinctly made in some of Strizhov's recent paintings.

It is possible to refer to a sense of abstraction about an image whereby the image holds a certain emphasis over the representational. Some of Strizhov's paintings approach this method. Three diverse, yet exemplary paintings fall into this category, namely, *The Thoughts of an Urban Bachelor, Prejudices of Copulating Insects,* and *White Oil Painting*. Although each is visually distinct in its approach to abstract reality (to borrow Mondrian's term), These paintings generally focus less on the narrative or symbolic aspect of the visual image and more on the nonobjective relationship between the shapes. This is not to suggest that they are exclusively formalist in their approach. Rather, it is to assert that the formal abstract elements within each artist signify a particular attitude or state of mind, an emotional state that has received a certain aesthetic distance.

Of the three paintings, *The Thoughts of an Urban Bachelor* still retains traces from the representational world. (I use this term to suggest a mimetic relationship to an externally perceived reality.) There are floating spherical heads, typical of the artist's style, a suggestion of a lower torso, a window perhaps, but generally the configuration is leaning more toward the abstract than the representation of an externally perceived reality. *Prejudices of Copulating Insects* is even more abstract in its pull away from external perception. It is an interior metaphysical painting, but also a humorous one, somewhere between the scale of Kandinsky and the content of Paul Klee. Another painting, entitled *Metaphysical Landscape,* is close in style and content to *Prejudices of Copulating Insects* and carries even greater complexity of form and color.

Untitled White Painting is unlike most of Strizhov's work. It is one of the few that has any trace of white. The shapes and lines, however, are clearly indicative of the artist's style. Then, of course, there is the problem with the application and appropriation of abstract shapes and designs within the context of Strizhov's paintings; this is the style of painting for which he is still best known and understood. It is where the content comes together with the form, where, as art theorist Rudolf Arnheim might say, the painting reaches a state of equilibrium, a necessary spatial tension and energetic reserve.

Dynamic Conversations

Here we should return for a moment to where this essay began—with

the subject of conversation. *Several Ways to Keep Up One's End of the*

Conversation is, of course, about a conversation. It is, however, not

only a conversation in the literal sense. It is also a conversation of

formal subject matter, that is, how the colors and shapes integrate

with each other to create a certain dynamic tension.

At least two people are needed for a conversation, which, in socio-

logical terminology, is known as a dyad. Dmitry Strizhov's paintings

are filled with such dyads—two-person groupings which somehow

imply that a language is being spoken or translated. Another paint-

ing, *A Dynamic Conversation,* suggests less diffidence than *Several Ways.*

One does not sense any reticence in this painting; there is no holding back. The two figures are approaching abstraction, without features. The third presence is a large-beaked mythological bird reminiscent of those painted by surrealists Juan Miro and Max Ernst. Although the two characters are faceless, the red background lends a peculiar energy to the event as if to transcribe the proceedings in the form of some kind of arcane ritual. It is an intense painting and extremely imaginative. There is also a kind of starkness about the shapes, an exuberance of color. The tension between the shapes and colors is evident, and this too becomes part of the formal conversation.

Another painting, *Walks Under a Northern Sky*, was also the title of Strizhov's CD of spoken poetry. (It is interesting to note that the late Poet Laureate, Joseph Brodsky, was one of Strizhov's main supporters in the artist's immigration to the United States.) In the painting, however, the two figures walk across the picture in elegant confidence. Just as there is a third party in *A Dynamic Conversation*, so too is there one in this painting—a large, smooth phallic dog. The painting suggests yet another type of conversation, one about wonder, searching out the words to explain what can never be perfectly explained: the mystery behind the creative process.

It would appear that with all the recent emphasis on theoretical constructs in academic courses on "visual culture" that little room is left to engage in what used to be called an "aesthetic experience."

Dmitry Strizhov is an artist who moves in the opposite (more open) direction. He is in search of a rich creative life where painting and language somehow manage to complement each other, even coalesce.

"Walks Under a Northern Sky" CD cover 1994
Dmitri Strizhov & Lou Christie & OBERMANEKEN

Walks Under a Northern Sky is a painting about wonderment. It reveals all the innocence of a mythic tale, and for this reason the painting contains a special power. This is not a matter of mystifying the work or the artist. It is merely one way of saying that painting is still able to communicate deep feelings through a sensual and conceptual means. Dmitry Strizhov has found his own way to deliver the mystery of life through art. How strange that this topic is rarely, if ever, discussed in art classes today. Regardless of this academic neglect, Strizhov is pursuing his own inner-directed course. It is a conflicted and enigmatic world, to be sure; but is it also a world in which the artist looks to the imagination as the rightful source for developing an extraordinary visual vocabulary. It is within this vocabulary that Strizhov enables us to discover the significance of feeling through art.

Color Plates

Man Obstructing a Portion of the Landscape. 1997 artist's collection.
Oil on Canvas, 50" x 44"

The Case of Katherine B. 1997 artist's collection.
Oil on Canvas, 50" x 44"

Answers Passing the Questions. 1993-1994 artist's collection.
Oil on Canvas, 48" x 40"

A Piece For Four Hands . 1997, artist's collection.
Oil on Canvas, 50" x 44"

Ballet. 1997 artist's collection.
Oil on Canvas, 44" x 50"

DJ D-Gree and His Daughter Stephanie in My Studio. 1997 artist's collection.
Oil on Canvas, 50" x 44"

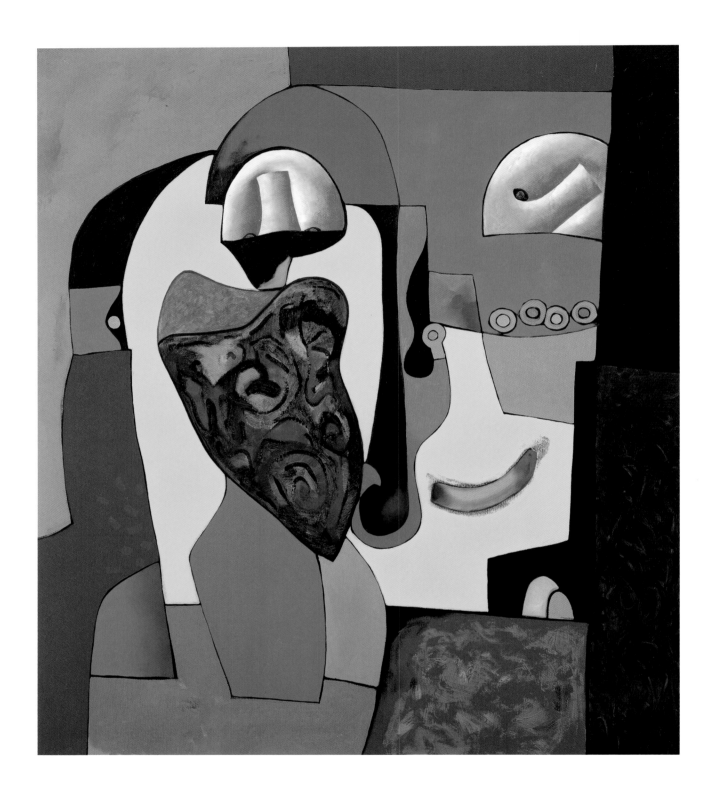

The Thoughts of an Urban Bachelor. 1997, artist's collection.
Oil on Canvas, 50" x 44"

Among the Flowers. 1994, collection of Steve Kaplan
Oil on Canvas, 31" x 40"

A Happy End of the Road. 1995, private collection, U.S.A.
Oil on Canvas, 50" x 50"

A Game With Shifting Mirrors. 1995, collection of Slava Golod, U.S.A.
Oil on Canvas, 44" x 50"

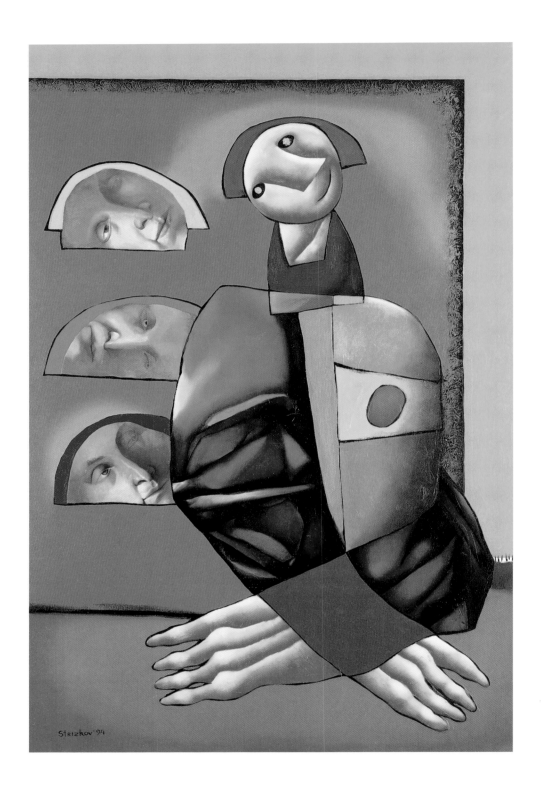

Face of the Dark Ages. 1994, collection of Mirek Nisenbaum, U.S.A.
Oil on Canvas, 48" x 32"

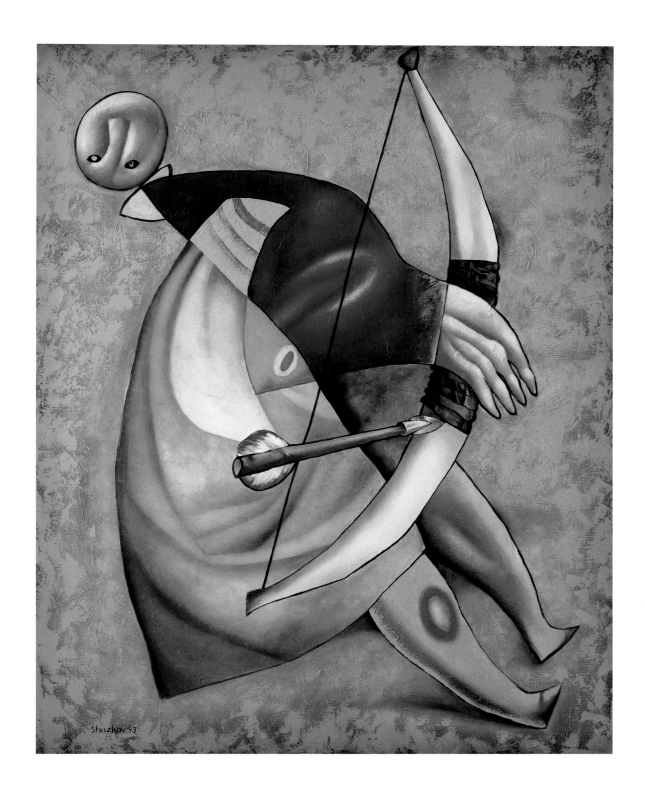

A Shot From A Bow. 1993, Private collection, Germany.
Oil on Canvas, 54" x 46"

Feathered Shadow on Black Road. 1997 artist's collection.
Oil on Canvas, 50" x 44"

Art History Written in Electricity. 1997 artist's collection.
Oil on Canvas, 50" x 44"

Green Bird and Yellow Mountain. 1994 artist's collection.
Oil on Canvas, 50" x 60"

Green Cat. 1997 artist's collection.
Oil on Canvas, 50" x 50"

Among the Colors of the Dark Ages. 1993, collection of David J. and Rhoda S. Narins, U.S.A.
Oil on Canvas, 48" x 34"

An Ancient Rock and its Owner. 1996. artist's collection.
Oil on Canvas, 44" x 50"

Lou Christie in an Italian City. 1995, private collection, U.S.A.
Oil on Canvas, 44" x 50"

Landscape with Alina. 1997, collection of Steve Kaplan.
Oil on Canvas, 50" x 44"

The Memorable Bits of a Blue Landscape. 1997 artist's collection.
Oil on Canvas, 50" x 44"

Yellow House. 1995, collection of Ilia Gorelik, U.S.A.
Oil on Canvas, 44" x 50"

Alina Summoning the Artist. 1997 artist's collection.
Oil on Canvas, 50" x 44"

Musician's Return to New York. 1996, collection of Lou Christie, U.S.A.
Oil on Canvas, 44" x 50"

St. Petersburg. 1997 artist's collection.
Oil on Canvas, 50" x 44"

Dog Pondering Katherine B. 1997 artist's collection.
Oil on Canvas, 44" x 50"

Metaphysical Landscape. 1997 artist's collection.
Oil on Canvas, 40" x 48"

Horse. 1997 artist's collection.
Oil on Canvas, 44" x 50"

An Enigmatic Mark in the Corner of the Painting. 1995 artist's collection.
Oil on Canvas, 50" x 58"

Dance. 1995 artist's collection.
Oil on Canvas, 50" x 44"

In Late Summer. 1992, private collection, U.S.A.
Oil on Canvas, 44" x 57"

Lou Christie Going Up the Staircase. 1994, collection of Lou Christie, U.S.A.
Oil on Canvas, 50" x 44"

Man with Green Hat. 1995, collection of Slava Golod, U.S.A.
Oil on Canvas, 44" x 50"

The Start of Sleep. 1997 artist's collection.
Oil on Canvas, 42" x 32"

Green Face. 1994, private collection. U.S.A.
Oil on Canvas, 44" x 50"

The Duration of the Note "A". 1995, collection of Eugene Ortenberg, U.S.A.
Oil on Canvas, 44" x 50"

Colored Line. 1993, private collection, England.
Oil on Canvas, 46" x 58"

The Level at Which Lines of this Painting Come Together by Themselves. 1993 artist's collection. Oil on Canvas, 46" x58"

Bookish Speech of Katherine B. 1992, private collection, England.
Oil on Canvas, 48" x 36"

Warrior of Dark Ages and his Thoughts. 1993, private collection, U.S.A.
Oil on Canvas, 46" x 40"

Yellow Moon. 1995, collection of Srdan Matic and Stella Sikic, U.S.A.
Oil on Canvas, 44" x 50"

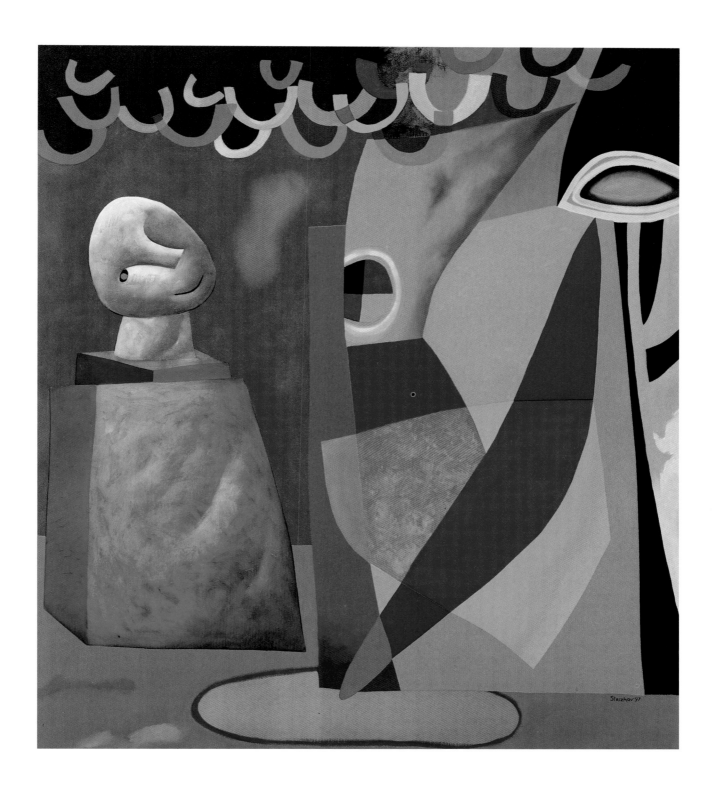

What Red and Blue Can Do. 1997, artist's collection.
Oil on Canvas, 50" x 44"

Additional Information On Reflections. 1997, artist's collection.
Oil on Canvas, 50" x 44"

A Few Things Riders Know. 1997, artist's collection.
Oil on Canvas, 44" x 50"

An Equdistant Word Combination 1994-1995, artist's collection.
Oil on Canvas, 50" x 64"

A Slip of Reflections. 1992, collection of David J. and Rhoda S. Narins, U.S.A.
Oil on Canvas, 54" x 66"

Classical Ballet. 1995-1996, artist's collection.
Oil on Canvas, 50" x 64"

Bird which Matches the Ladder. 1997, artist's collection.
Oil on Canvas, 44" x 50"

Strizhov'97

Sculptors. 1991, private collection, U.S.A.
Oil on Canvas, 50" x 64"

Hunter of the Dark Ages. 1993, artist's collection.
Oil on Canvas, 46" x 54"

Musician with French Horn. 1993, private collection, U.S.A.
Oil on Canvas, 54" x 48"

My Life in Novel Forms. 1993-1997, artist's collection.
Oil on Canvas, 50" x 56"

Man With Pipe. 1993, private collection, England.
Oil on Canvas, 48" x 34"

Prejudices of Copulating Insects. 1996-1997, artist's collection.
Oil on Canvas, 48" x 60"

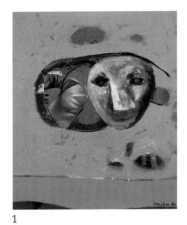

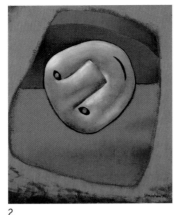

1

2

3

1) **Yellow Jacket.** 1994, private collection, U.S.A.
Oil on Canvas, 24" x 18"

2) **Green Head.** 1994, collection of Jennifer Tim, U.S.A.
Oil on Canvas, 20" x 16"

3) **The Notebook of Artist.** 1994.
Oil on Canvas, 21" x 16"

4

5

6

4) **Red Line.** 1994, private collection, U.S.A.
Oil on Canvas, 24" x 18"

5) **The Start of Dream.** 1994,
collection of Semion and Lucy Pesochinsky, U.S.A.
Oil on Canvas, 20" x 16"

6) **New Face.** 1994.
Oil on Canvas, 21" x 16"

7

8

9

7) **What Gray and Blue Can Do.** 1994,
private collection, Israel.
Oil on Canvas, 34" x 20"

8) **What Green and Yellow Can Do.** 1994,
private collection, Jakarta.
Oil on Canvas, 24" x 18"

9) **Music Exclusive of it's Notes.** 1994,
artist's collection.
Oil on Canvas, 30" x 22"

1) **Katherine B's Touch.** 1995,
Oil on Canvas, 16" x 22"

2) **Art History Written in Sound.** 1997,
Oil on Canvas, 20" x 20"

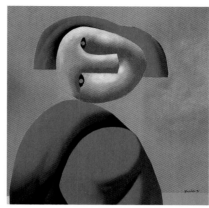

1

2

3) **Stones Within Which Shadows Hide.** 1995,
artist's collection.
Oil on Canvas, 19" x 24"

3

Stones Left As They Are. 1993,
collection of David J. and Rhoda S. Narins, U.S.A.
Oil on Canvas, 28" x 40"

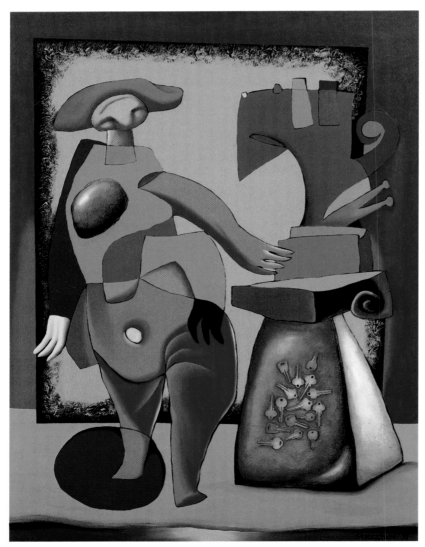

The Property of Certain Shapes. 1991,
collection of Mary Hansen and Chris Pfeifer.
Oil on Canvas, 48" x 36"

Man with red bird. 1993, artist's collection.
Oil on Canvas, 30" x 35"

Red Oil Painting. 1992, collection of Vlad Tolmachiov, U.S.A.
Oil on Canvas, 40" x 30"

Conversation. 1993, Edwin-Scharff-Haus Museum, Germany.
Oil on Canvas, 44" x 50"

Color TV. 1995, private collection, Germany.
Oil on Canvas, 40" x 54"

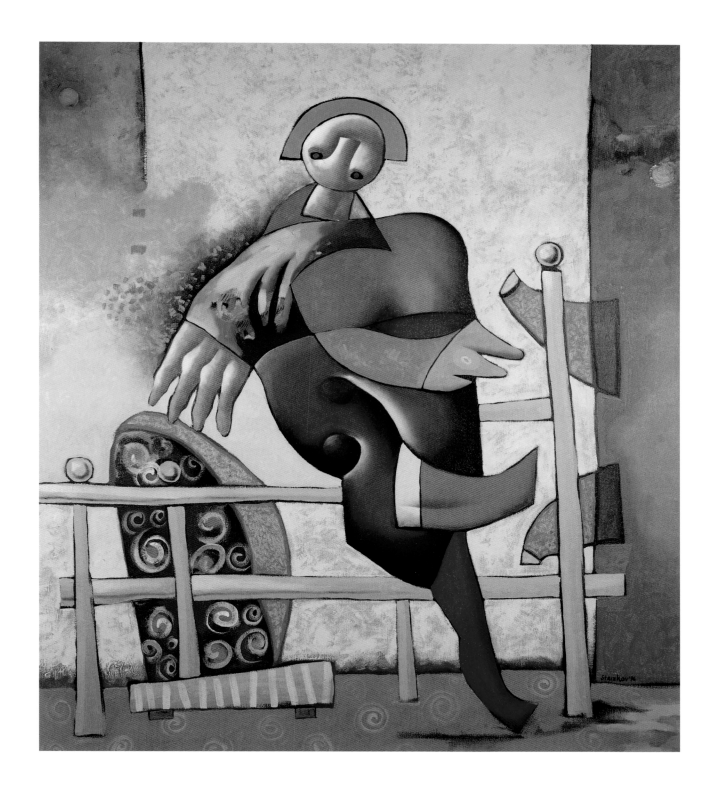

Dancer. 1996, private collection, U.S.A.
Oil on Canvas, 50" x 44"

Nearby Yellow Stone. 1995, private collection, U.S.A.
Oil on Canvas, 44" x 50"

First Day of Autumn. 1993, private collection, U.S.A.
Oil on Canvas, 50" x 64"

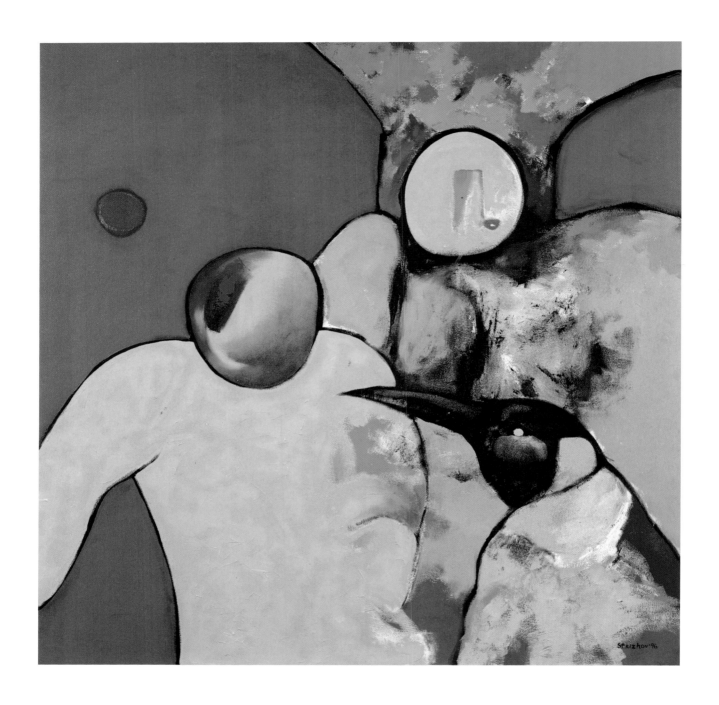

A Dynamic Conversation. 1996, artist's collection.
Oil on Canvas, 40" x 40"

Lou Christie Picking Out A Color Chord. 1996, artist's collection.
Oil on Canvas, 44" x 50"

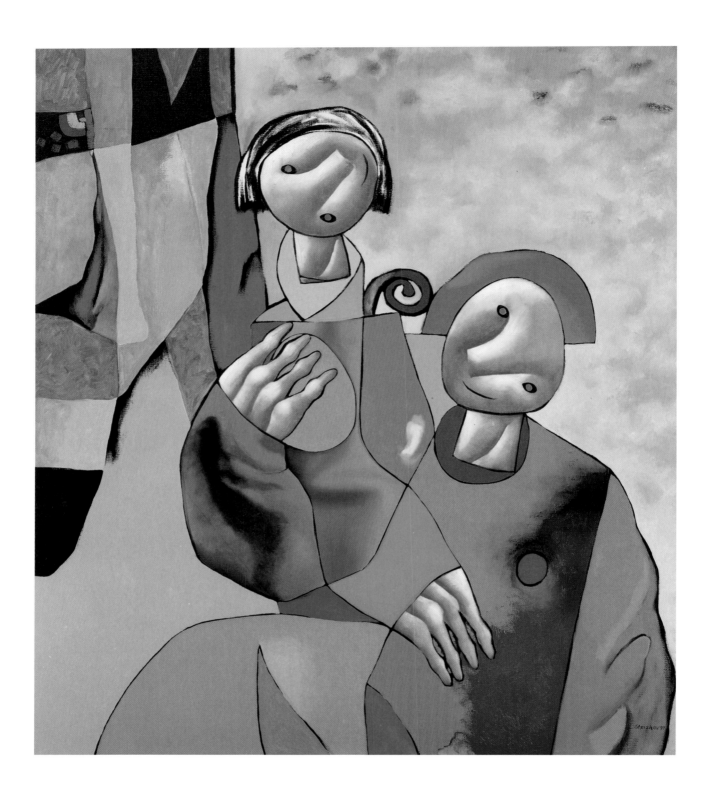

Several Ways to Keep Up One's End of the Conversation. 1997, artist's collection.
Oil on Canvas, 50" x 44"

Orange Cat. 1991, artist's collection.
Oil on Canvas, 54" x 66"

Revelry on the Level of Historic Days. 1992, artist's collection.
Oil on Canvas, 54" x 66"

White Oil Painting. 1994, artist's collection.
Oil on Canvas, 54" x 66"

Musicians Playing for Alina. 1997, artist's collection.
Oil on Canvas, 50" x 44"

Blue Sofa. 1994, collection of Ilya Garelic, U.S.A.
Oil on Canvas, 50" x 64"

Man Possessing a Cubic Still Life. 1997, artist's collection.
Oil on Canvas, 50" x 44"

The Builder's Artistic Nature. 1997, artist's collection.
Oil on Canvas, 50" x 44"

A Painting Which Remains Unnamed. 1994, artist's collection.
Oil on Canvas, 58" x 40"

Strizhov '94

Fish With Blue Tale. 1995, collection of Ilya Garelic, U.S.A.
Oil on Canvas, 34" x 28"

Artist in His Studio. 1993, collection of K. Kuzminsky, U.S.A.
Oil on Canvas, 20" x 30"

Man With an Exaggerated SENSE of Proportion. 1993, artist's collection.
Oil on Canvas, 50" x 44"

The Automotive Cloud and its Role in Interior Design. 1997, artist's collection.
Oil on Canvas, 50" x 44"

Impressions Of Certain Books. 1992, collection of Elena Tschernischova, U.S.A.
Oil on Canvas, 52" x 50"

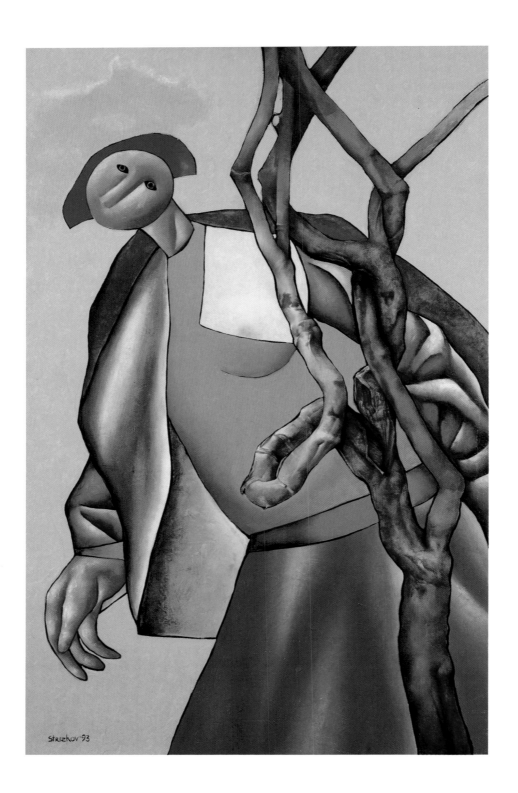

Alina in Conversation with Katherine B. 1993, artist's collection.
Oil on Canvas, 48" x 30"

An Album of Salvador Dali Without Illustrations. 1995, private collection, U.S.A.
Oil on Canvas, 44" x 50"

Displacement of Blue Sound. 1995, Collection of Mark Hutchins, U.S.A.
Oil on Canvas, 50" x 44"

Man With Accordion. 1993, Collection of Judith and Martin Feingold, U.S.A.
Oil on Canvas, 50" x 44"

Art History Written in Movement. 1992, Private collection, Germany.
Oil on Canvas, 54" x 66"

Brown Bag. 1993, Private collection, U.S.A.
Oil on Canvas, 50" x 44"

Central Park. 1993, artist's collection.
Oil on Canvas, 48" x 38"

City in Which it is Already Night. 1991, private collection, U.S.A.
Oil on Canvas, 48" x 38"

Landscape. 1994, Private collection. U.S.A.
Oil on Canvas, 50" x 44"

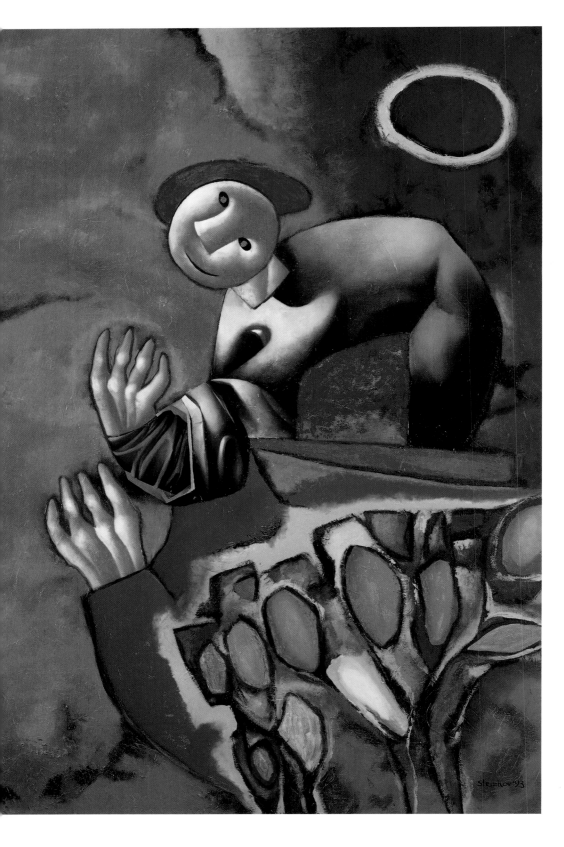

Green Circle. 1993, Edwin-Scharff-Haus Museum, Germany.
Oil on Canvas, 54" x 46"

Far From Bruegel. 1995, Collection of Diane K. Wilson, U.S.A.
Oil on Canvas, 50" x 64"

History of Art, Underground. 1992, private collection, U.S.A.
Oil on Canvas, 60" x 72"

Holidays and Their Devotees. 1997, artist's collection.
Oil on Canvas, 48" x 44"

In a Grecian Hall. 1997, artist's collection.
Oil on Canvas, 50" x 44"

Man With Violet Horn. 1995, Collection of Michael Ioffe, U.S.A.
Oil on Canvas, 50" x 44"

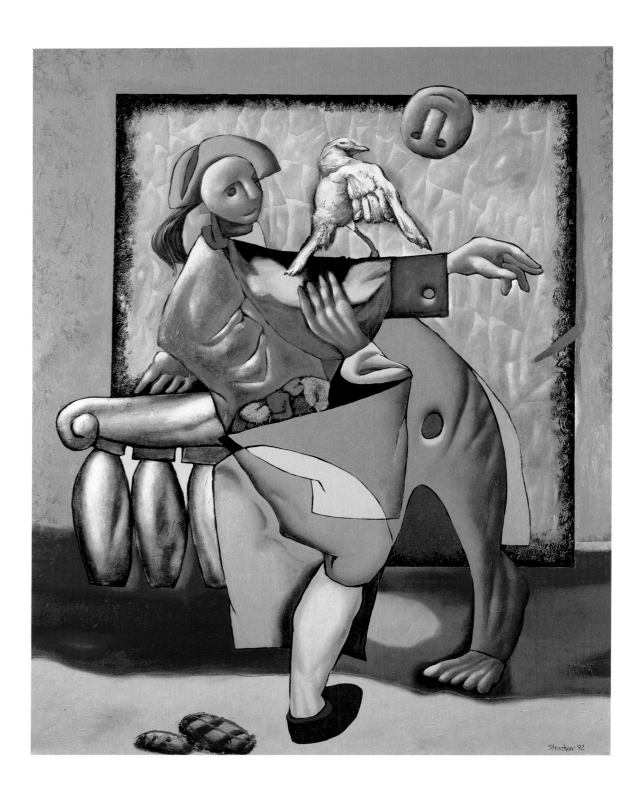

Man with a Bird. 1992, private collection. U.S.A.
Oil on Canvas, 66" x 54"

Green Oil Painting. 1996, artist's collection.
Oil on Canvas, 48" x 60"

Little Plant. 1995, private collection, Germany.
Oil on Canvas, 44" x 50"

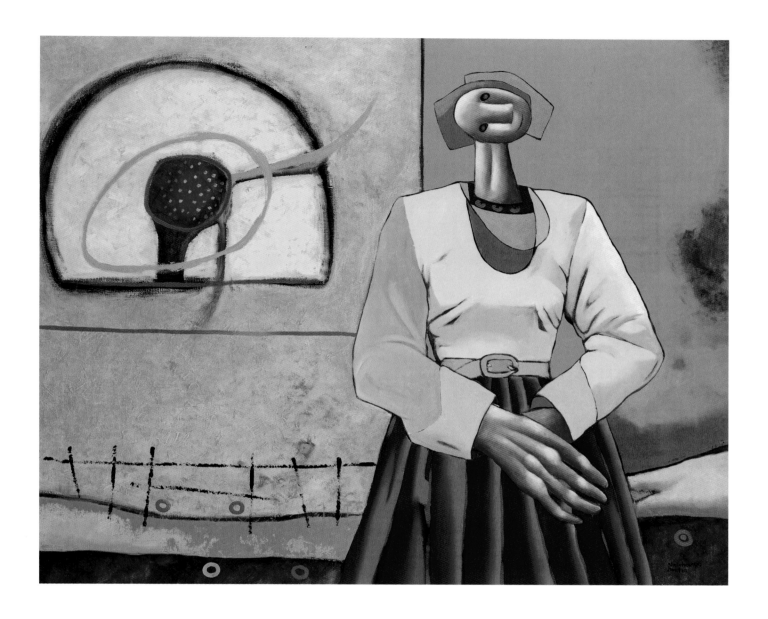

KatherineB In Green. 1995, artist's collection.
Oil on Canvas, 40" x 48"

Man with the Green Pear. 1993, Edwin-Scharff-Haus Museum, Germany.
Oil on Canvas, 52" x 50"

Man and a Dynamic Landscape. 1995, artist's collection.
Oil on Canvas, 38" x 57"

Man with Blue Circle. 1997, artist's collection.
Oil on Canvas, 44" x 50"

Man with Scissors and Oranges. 1993, artist's collection.
Oil on Canvas, 44" x 50"

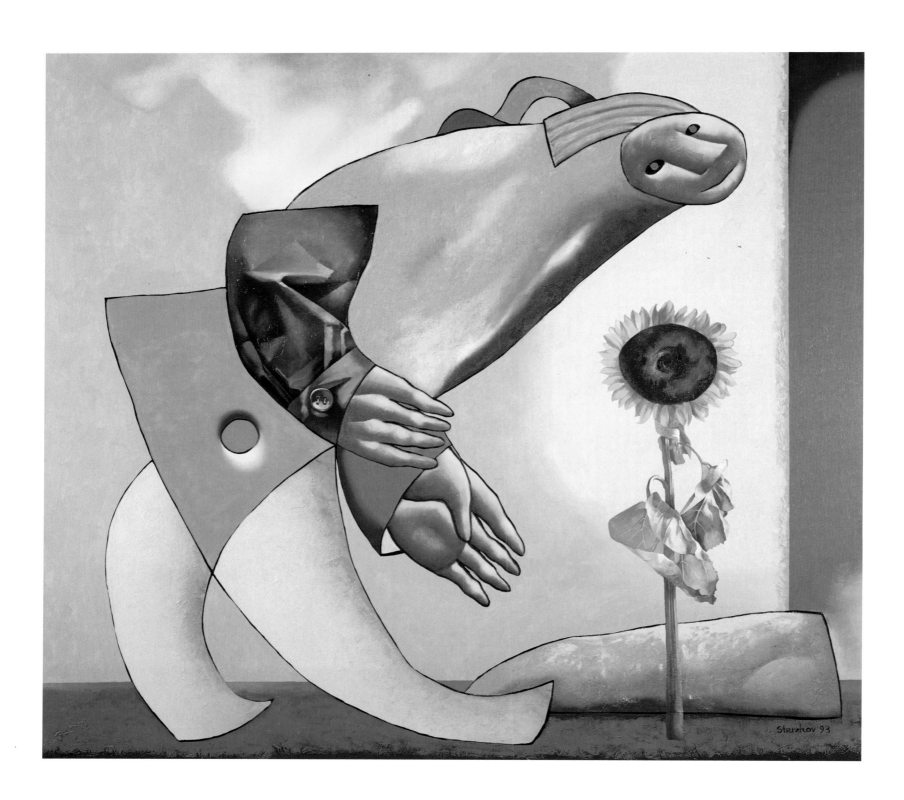

Man with Sunflower. 1993, private collection. U.S.A.
Oil on Canvas, 44" x 50"

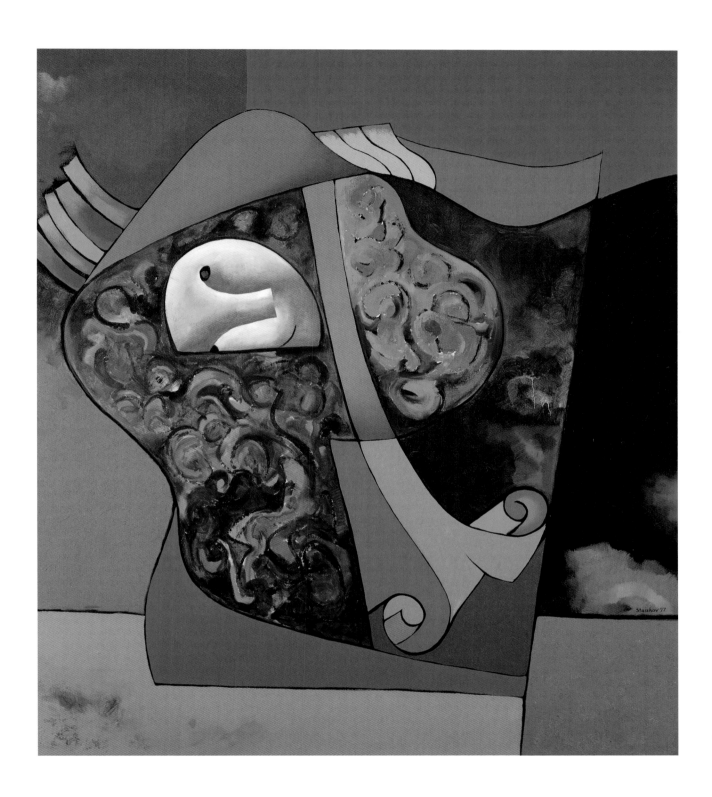

Modesty of Alina. 1997, artist's collection.
Oil on Canvas, 50" x 44"

Metaphysical Beast. 1996, artist's collection.
Oil on Canvas, 50" x 68"

Moving Backwards. 1994, private collection, U.S.A.
Oil on Canvas, 44" x 50"

Musician. 1993, private collection, Switzerland.
Oil on Canvas, 44" x 50"

She sings as though I'd know how to
To play her an accompaniment.
As if I'd know how to brighten
Any play with her music....

Strizhov 93

Musician Playing for Pink Face. 1993, collection of Doran Nissan, U.S.A.
Oil on Canvas, 54" x 66"

Painting Conversing with its Owner. 1997, artist's collection.
Oil on Canvas, 50" x 44"

Parting With Katherine B. 1992, private collection, U.S.A.
Oil on Canvas, 54" x 66"

People Jumping out of Bags. 1997, artist's collection.
Oil on Canvas, 50" x 44"

Rolling Chair. 1997, private collection, Germany.
Oil on Canvas, 44" x 50"

Pink Oil Painting. 1996, collection of Dmitri Tcherniavski
Oil on Canvas, 44" x 50"

Power of Flashlight. 1995, private collection, U.S.A.
Oil on Canvas, 44" x 50"

Red Sky. 1994, collection of Anatole Plotkin, U.S.A.
Oil on Canvas, 50" x 44"

Alina in Old City. 1997, artist's collection.
Oil on Canvas, 50" x 44"

Reflecting Table. 1993, private collection, U.S.A.
Oil on Canvas, 54" x 48"

Simple Objects in Katherine B's Hands. 1997, artist's collection.
Oil on Canvas, 44" x 50"

Simplified Still Life. 1997, artist's collection.
Oil on Canvas, 44" x 50"

Spanish Man. 1997, artist's collection.
Oil on Canvas, 50" x 44"

Still Life. 1993, Edwin-Scharff-Haus Museum, Germany.
Oil on Canvas, 32" x 38"

Still Life of Katherin B. 1993, private collection, Germany.
Oil on Canvas, 44" x 50"

Stone & Paper. 1993, private collection, Germany
Oil on Canvas, 40" x 48"

The First to Paint as I do. 1991, private collection, U.S.A.
Oil on Canvas, 50" x 66"

The Advent of Red Sound. 1997, artist's collection.
Oil on Canvas, 48" x 60"

The Execution of the Fourth Desire. 1992, private collection, U.S.A.
Oil on Canvas, 54" x 66"

The Cubic Motion of the Fisherman. 1997, artist's collection.
Oil on Canvas, 44" x 50"

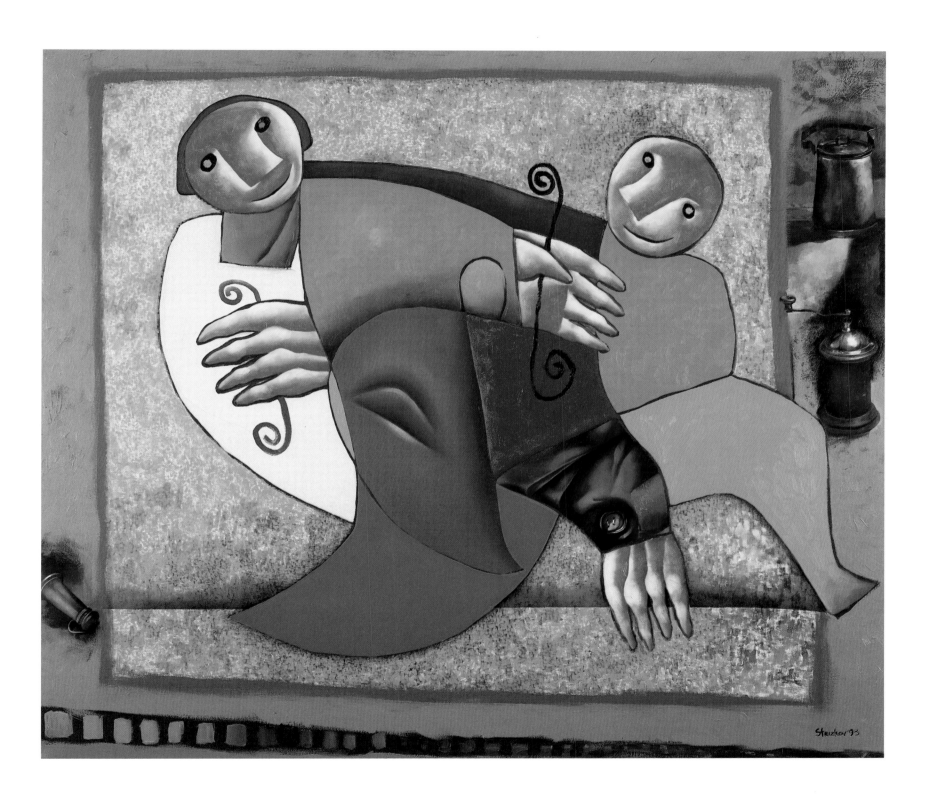

The Meaning of the Second Word. 1993, private collection, Germany.
Oil on Canvas, 54" x 66"

The Return of Red Color. 1996, private collection, U.S.A.
Oil on Canvas, 44" x 50"

The Thoughts of an Urban Horseman. 1995, private collection, U.S.A.
Oil on Canvas, 66" x 60"

The Simplicity of the Astonishing Falls of Katherine B. 1997, artist's collection.
Oil on Canvas, 50" x 44"

Three Flowers. 1993, private collection. Germany.
Oil on Canvas, 44" x 50"

Together. 1995, private collection, U.S.A.
Oil on Canvas, 50" x 64"

The Tranquil World of Still Life. 1997, artist's collection.
Oil on Canvas, 50" x 44"

The Tranquil World of the Landscape. 1997, artist's collection.
Oil on Canvas, 50" x 44"

Touching the Later Books. 1993, private collection, U.S.A.
Oil on Canvas, 54" x 66"

Woman Carrying Jugs. 1996, artist's collection.
Oil on Canvas, 50" x 52"

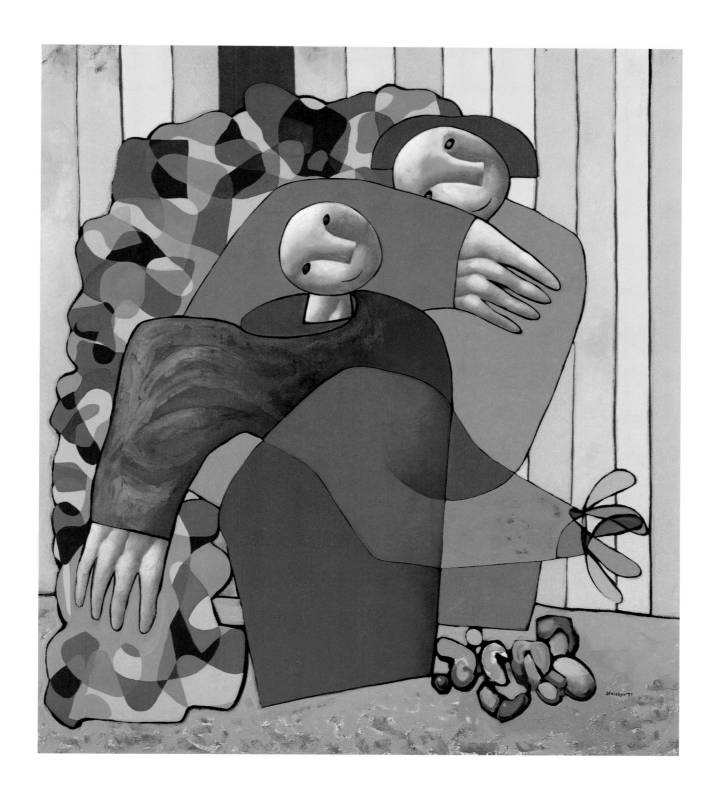

Unfamiliar Contrasts. 1997, artist's collection.
Oil on Canvas, 50" x 44"

Woman Carrying Mirror. 1996, private collection, U.S.A.
Oil on Canvas, 50" x 44"

Walks Under a Northern Sky. 1993, artist's collection.
Oil on Canvas, 54" x 66"

Woman With Cat. 1997, artist's collection.
Oil on Canvas, 44" x 50"

On the Edge of Katherine B's Pupil. 1992,
collection of Keng Chun Chen
Oil on Canvas, 54" x 66"

Color Relationship with Katherine B. 1991,
artist's collection.
Oil on Canvas, 54" x 66"

Woman With a Bird. 1992, private collection, U.S.A.
Oil on Canvas, 54" x 66"

Woman with a Masque. 1991, private collection, U.S.A.
Oil on Canvas, 54" x 66"

Yellow Circle. 1995, private collection, England.
Oil on Canvas, 44" x 50"

Yellow Sky. 1995, artist's collection.
Oil on Canvas, 50" x 64"

Yellow and Blue Sky. 1995, private collection, England.
Oil on Canvas, 34" x 44"

A Few Red Points. 1995, artist's collection.
Oil on Canvas, 50" x 36"

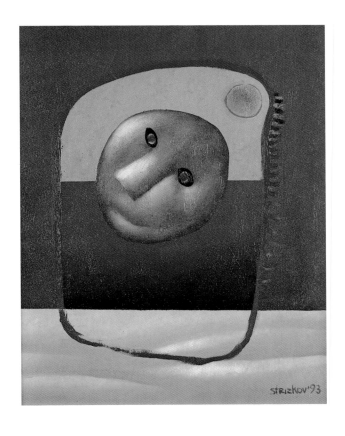

Blue Contour. 1993, private collection, U.S.A.
Oil on Canvas, 24" x 18"

Yellow Line. 1994, private collection, Germany.
Oil on Canvas, 26" x 19"

Blue Sky. 1993, private collection, Germany.
Oil on Canvas, 35" x 44"

Green Fish. 1996, private collection, U.S.A.
Oil on Canvas, 36" x 36"

Green Hat. 1992, private collection, U.S.A.
Oil on Canvas, 30" x 48"

Green Light. 1995, private collection, U.S.A.
Oil on Canvas, 48" x 54"

Pink Flower. 1993, private collection. U.S.A.
Oil on Canvas, 30" x 44"

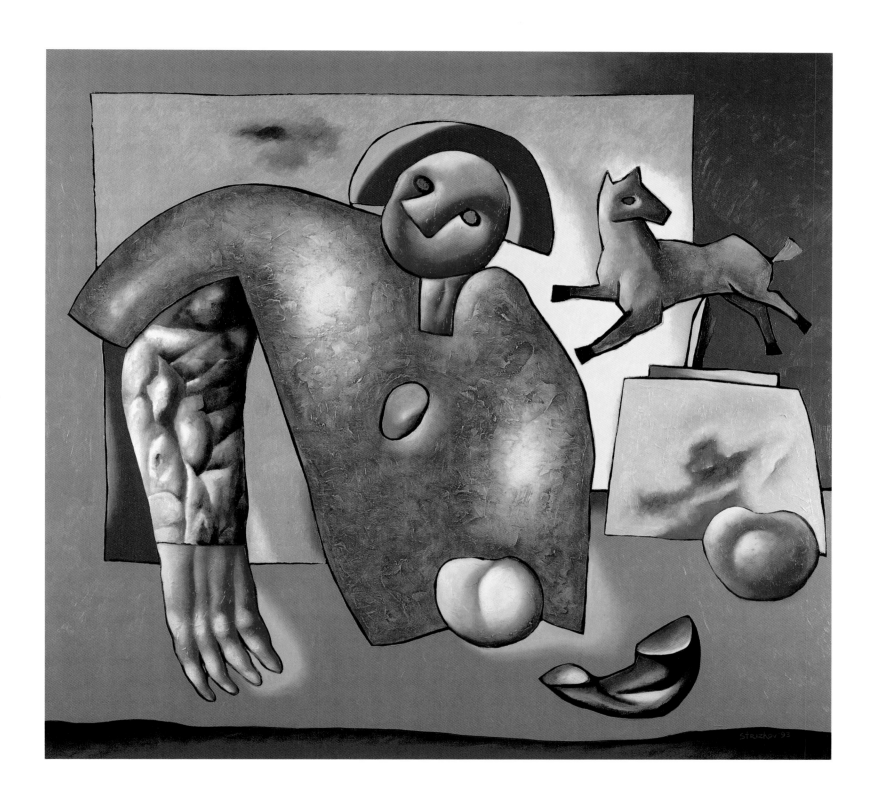

Red Peach. 1993, private collection, U.S.A.
Oil on Canvas, 36″ x 38″

Red Stairs. 1994, private collection, U.S.A.
Oil on Canvas, 44" x 50"

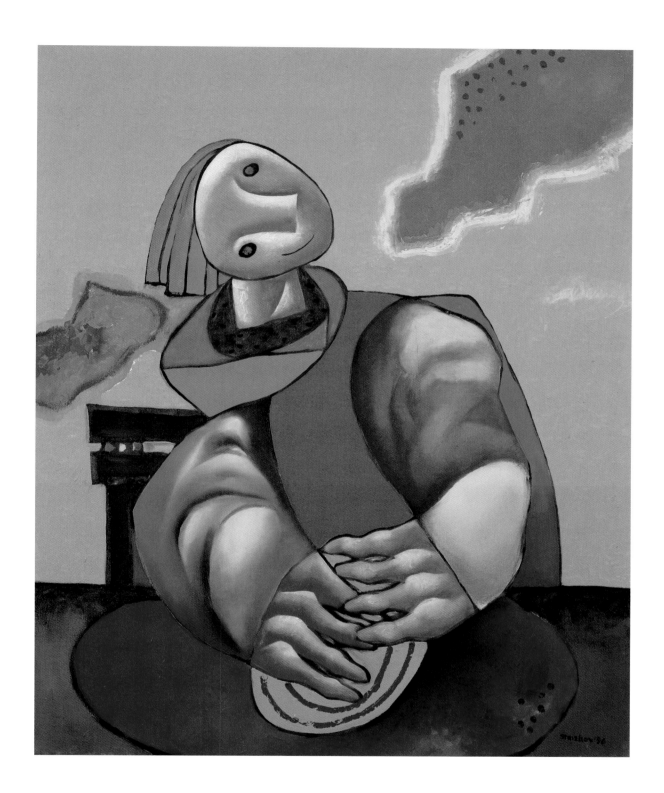

Red Table. 1996, artist's collection.
Oil on Canvas, 38" x 32"

Biography and Chronology

1967	Born in Leningrad (St. Petersburg), Russia.
1979-84	High School of Fine Art at Academy of Arts.
1984	Graduated from the Leningrad School of Fine Arts.
1988	Joined the Leningrad Union of Free Artisits, the first independent group of its kind.
1990	Moves to New York City, U.S.A.

E x h i b i t i o n s

1990	Leningrad Union of Free Artists Gallery, Soviet Union.
	Exhibition, West Berlin, Germany.
1991	Ergane Gallery, New York, U.S.A.
	Albright -Knox Art Gallery, Buffalo, NY.
	Robert Dana Gallery, San Francisco.
1992	Completes commissioned stage sets for Danbury Music Center's annual production of "Nutcracker".
	Commissioned stage sets, curtain and poster for Vienna State Ballet's production of "Don Quixote".
1993	"The color Relationship with Katherine B., "Ergane Gallery, New York, U.S.A. "Formal Limitations of Figuration and Abstraction", Edwin-Scharff-Haus Museum, Neu-Ulm, Germany. "Advant-Grade Oils" Robert Dana Gallery, San Francisco, CA.
1994	"Pictures Painted to the Music of Katherine B.", Develine Gallery, New York, U.S.A.
	R & R Gallery, Stanford, Connecticut.
1995	Develine Gallery, New York, U.S.A.
1996	The Gettysburg College Gallery
	Savva Gallery, New York, U.S.A.
1997	Commissioned stage sets for Merrian Theater The Univercity of the Arts, Philadelphia. Savva Gallery, New York, U.S.A.